Rookie
Read-About Science®

Frie... Dolphins

By Allan Fowler

Consultants
Linda Cornwell, Learning Resource Consultant,
Indiana Department of Education

Fay Robinson, Child Development Specialist

Children's Press®
A Division of Grolier Publishing
New York   London   Hong Kong   Sydney
Danbury, Connecticut

Project Editor: Downing Publishing Services
Designer: Herman Adler Design Group
Photo Researcher: Caroline Anderson

Library of Congress Cataloging-in-Publication Data

Fowler, Allan.
    Friendly dolphins / by Allan Fowler.
        p. cm. – (Rookie read-about science)
    Includes index.
    Summary: Briefly describes the physical characteristics and behavior of
dolphins and several related marine mammals, killer whales, and porpoises.
    ISBN 0-516-20428-9 (lib. bdg.)   0-516-26256-4 (pbk.)
    1. Dolphins—Juvenile literature.   2. Killer whales—Juvenile literature.
3. Porpoises—Juvenile literature. [1. Dolphins.] I. Title. II. Series.
QL737.C432F68   1997   96-46953
599.53—dc21   CIP
                                                                    AC

With their big smiles,
dolphins look friendly.
And they are friendly.
Frisky, too.

Dolphins perform in shows
at aquariums, marine parks,
and theme parks.

They gladly let people
pat their backs or rub
their bellies.

They can be trained to wave
"hello" with their flippers.
They play ball . . .

leap high out of the
water . . . even "walk"
or "dance" on their tails.

Dolphins sometimes swim ahead of ships, guiding them safely into port.

Dolphins have saved people from drowning.

A swimmer in trouble may be gently pushed ashore by an alert dolphin.

The dolphins you usually
see in shows are bottlenose
dolphins. They are about
6 to 12 feet long.

Spotted dolphins and
common dolphins are
a little smaller.

But a marine mammal
could be as much as 30 feet
long . . . and be called an
orca, or killer whale . . . and
it could still be a dolphin.

All dolphins are members
of the whale family.

An orca is really a kind of
dolphin. It looks different
from other dolphins because
it's so much bigger.

Unlike most dolphins,
it has a white belly.

Why are orcas also called
killer whales? In the ocean,
they eat fish, seals, birds —
even other dolphins.

Packs of killer whales will attack large whales. But they have never been known to attack people.

Orcas perform at marine parks. When trained, they are just as clever, and just as friendly, as bottlenose dolphins.

Here's how high an orca can leap. Imagine the splash it will make when it comes down. If you were sitting in the front rows, you'd get all wet.

If you live near the Atlantic or Pacific Coast, you may have seen porpoises in a harbor, playfully jumping and rolling.

Like dolphins, porpoises are members of the whale family.

They are a bit smaller than dolphins.

Porpoises have rounded snouts, but dolphins have long, pointy snouts.

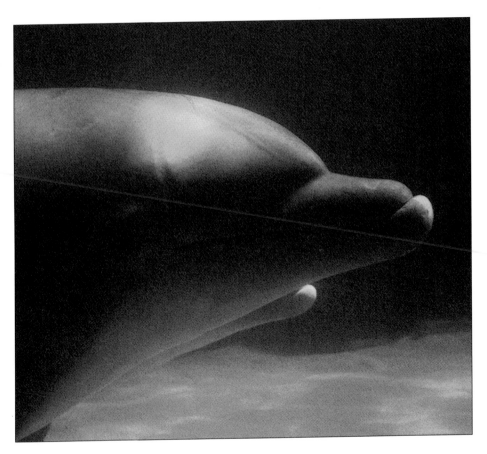

All dolphins can stay
underwater a long time.
They are not fish, though
— they are mammals.

They must come to the
surface and breathe air,
through blowholes on
top of their heads.

Fish breathe underwater, through slits called gills.

Dolphins swim by
moving their tails, or
flukes, up and down
in a wavy motion.

Like other whales, dolphins seem to "talk" among themselves with chirps and squeals.

Dolphins used to be killed
by tuna-fishing crews.

They thought the dolphins
were eating too many tunas.

Dolphins also became
accidentally snagged in
the tuna nets. But dolphins
are protected now.

Next time you eat tuna, look at the can. It should say something like "Dolphin Safe." That means the fishing crews were careful not to kill any dolphins.

It's good to know there
will always be dolphins —
smiling, chattering, leaping,
and just being friendly.

Words You Know

bottlenose dolphin

common dolphin

spotted dolphin

orca (killer whale)

marine park

blowhole

flipper

fluke (tail)

Index

About the Author

Allan Fowler is a free-lance writer with a background in advertising.
Born in New York, he lives in Chicago now and enjoys traveling.

Photo Credits

©: Marine Mammal Images: 7 (ACS-G Baker), 15 (Kelly Balcomb-Bartock), 21 (Mark Conlin), 9 (Thomas Henninsen), 25 (Michael Nolan), 6 (Eda Rogers), 31 bottom center (James Watt); Norbert Wu Photography: 4, 31 top, 31 bottom right; Peter Arnold Inc.: 11, 29, 30 top right, 30 bottom left (Kelvin Altken), cover (S.J. Krasemann), 10 (Gerard Lacz), 28 (Leonard Lessin), 14 (David McNew), 22 (Steven Morello), 3, 30 top left (Roland Seitre); Superstock, Inc.: 13, 23, 27, 30 bottom right; Visuals Unlimited: 17, 20 (John D. Cunningham), 5 (Ken Lucas), 18 (Robert M. Peck), 31 bottom left (Gary Robinson), 24 (Marty Snyderman).